Desire Zoo

Desire ZOO

POEMS

ALISON
LUTERMAN

TIA CHUCHA PRESS

For Sophie,
Thank you for
being such a
good support to
Angela —
All my best,
Alison

ISBN 978-1-882688-47-0

Book design: Jane Brunette
Cover image: Lauren Ari, "The Spark Between"

Published by:
Tia Chucha Press
A project of Tia Chucha's Centro Cultural & Bookstore
PO Box 328
San Fernando CA 91341

Distributed by:
Northwestern University Press
Chicago Distribution Center
11030 S. Langley
Chicago IL 60628

Tia Chucha's Centro Cultural & Bookstore is a 501 (c) (3) tax-exempt organization
supported by the California Community Foundation, California Arts Council, Los
Angeles County Arts Commission, Los Angeles City Department of Cultural Affairs,
the Annenberg Foundation, the Lia Fund, the Attias Family Foundation, the Gua-
camole Fund, and the Weingart Foundation, among others. And donations from
Bruce Springsteen, John Densmore of The Doors, Jackson Brown, Lou Adler, Richard
Foos, Gary Stewart, Luis and Trini Rodriguez, and more.

for Lee Bates

CONTENTS

3 Honeymouth

1

MAN ON WIRE,
WOMAN ON COUCH,
SCREAMING

Young Buck on Snake Road

What was he doing there,
the young buck, clip-clopping
nervously down Snake Road,
his antlers held at a rakish angle?
Five o'clock sunset, November,
and the low beams shooting
through my dusty windshield.
I crawled slowly
behind him, holding my breath.
Sometimes Zeus comes down in a shower of gold,
sometimes as a stag who has wandered off course,
nibbling in forbidden gardens.
I'd been gardening all day, sixteen bucks
an hour, all cash, crammed in my pocket,
my back beginning to seize up,
the knees of my jeans caked
and cracked with mud.
I believe every movement
we make is recorded:
stooping, kneeling, bending, pulling—
and I'm not talking about god.
I'm talking ligament, fascia and muscle.
The tender body of the world.
That afternoon we'd cleared weeds
and leaf-litter off a steep hillside,
then sprinkled dried dung over native ground cover
until it buzzed with flies like a live thing.
A day like this lets you know
everything is alive, even
the dust streaks on my windshield
as I grip the steering wheel, inching
slowly down Snake Road after the deer
like the lead car in a retinue

following a prince. What if I'd
sped thoughtless around that bend and hit him?
At the corner of Colton he turned right
and I continued down Thornhill,
the sun a low flaming frisbee in the sky,
the brightness of everything just about blinding me.

Man On Wire, Woman On Couch, Screaming

Watching a film about Philippe Petit wire-walking
between the twin towers of the World Trade Center

Above flapping green awnings and cars idling at stoplights,
above yellow lines and white lines painted on asphalt,
and the man hawking coffee and donuts from his little metal cart—

Above cruel, jagged cornices of buildings.
Above clouds, above gulls and their squawking.
Higher than that.
A hundred and ten stories up—

one slippered foot glides onto a strung cable, then the other,
and he's dancing, holding nothing
but a long pole, balanced against air currents,
against laws, against common sense,
dancing in God's empty palm.

Slender wisp of a man.   Black-clad crazy clown.
And you, watching the video on your couch,
why are you screaming and writhing
like a woman in orgasm or childbirth, like someone being dangled
head-down from a great height?

You're safe as a hamster in your own safe house,
watching this man walk on a wire between what used to be
twin towers—there used to be a world to step off from:
elevators, fax machines, water coolers.
Who'd ever dream the dreamer would outlast steel?

There are moments you pray to be ready for
but seldom are.
He steps off the edge into air.

Great shining panes of light: sheer freedom.
The magnetic dread and pull of it.
Now he kneels. Now he salutes
the towers, the city, all space and time.
Now he lies down,
face to the sky, perfectly relaxed,
and you want to faint,
you who do not trust even the ground
to hold you, who think you'll fall
off the earth for one misspoken word—

But this.
It's like being inside a cathedral
of pure terror,
skewered by the sound of bells.

And even after he climbs down
and is received into the blue-coated arms
of a New York City cop;
even after the whole city exhales
and goes back to its ordinary pleasures and ills—

it goes on, somewhere, forever in the mind, in the living cells.
To step out of the possible
into amazement. How the dream floats
over the city
where steel melted and buildings dissolved;

how in the end only the ephemeral
endures.

Because These Failures Are My Job

This morning I failed to notice the pearl-gray moment
just before sunrise when everything lightens;
failed also to find bird song under the grinding of garbage trucks,
and later, walking through woods, to stop thinking, thinking
for even five consecutive steps. Then there was the failure to name
the exact shade of blue overhead, not sapphire, not azure, not Delft,
to savor the soft squelch of pine needles underfoot.
Later I found the fork raised halfway to my mouth
while I was still chewing the last untasted bite.
And so it went, until finally, wading into sleep's thick undertow,
I felt myself drift from dream to dream,
forever failing to comprehend where I am falling from or to:
this blurred life with only moments caught
in attention's loose sieve —
tiny pearls fished out of oblivion's sea
laid out here as offering or apology or thank you

Pausing Before Plunging In

But I never do.
Marriages, voyages, the ocean.
It's cold, vast, stinks of fish.
You can feel the briny chill of it
the way you can feel the warmth of a person's mouth
before you kiss them,
a puff of garlic or coffee, a whiff of yeasty beer,
and from that moment, a whole life:
grocery bags, raked leaves,
flossing at night, jostling
for space in front of the same mirror.
Late-afternoon sun plummets into the West,
rises just as quickly, turns
from streaking dawn clouds
to floods and floods of light,
a tsunami of gold.
You can say stealing shadows,
you can say gradual thaw,
or drip, drip, drip,
but the one chosen sperm doesn't hesitate
when faced with the looming
moonrise of egg.
It just darts right in
as if it belonged there,
leaving tail, fins, and animal caution behind.

Love Shack

The only room in the house we can heat properly becomes the only room where I'll let you undress me. You drag the mattress over by the radiator and we become two teenagers, doing it on the floor of the den where no one can hear us. Welcome to the love shack, you say, unbuttoning your shirt. You look like an eager cowboy with his first woman. Outside, the persimmon tree is losing the last of its rusty leaves. The peach trees are already bare and witch-like, the lemon tree shivers in the cold rain. In here, it's warming up. I'm wearing the sapphire dress and black tights. You want me with my dress on, then you lift it over my head. Our long pale limbs flush the color the magnolia blossoms will be in a few months. Your face gets hot, your lips loose and wet and soft like a boy. We are going back, going back, through the detritus of adulthood, marriages to other people, jobs, journeys when the car broke down, when the check bounced, when nobody came to the rescue. And then younger, the lonely brilliant teenage years, me writing poetry fanatically in my room, you teaching yourself Beethoven by force of will, practicing without a teacher, rudderless. There is no teacher for this. I've heard the stories of your childhood, roaming over the hills and vacant lots in suburban Michigan. That land has all been bulldozed. I imagine your mother pushing you out of her, headfirst into this crazy world. I am stroking the hair back from your sweaty forehead and whispering Baby.

.

Arrow

Carla, whom I refuse to believe
is dying, says, *And another thing.*
Love the fuck out of whomever you love.
I'm serious as a heart attack,
she insists, punching a button
on her motorized wheelchair. I keep an eye out;
last month she went joy-riding,
crashed into a wall, and broke her toe.
And have sex, plenty of sex,
as much as you can, while you can, she instructs.
Her gaze is direct, letting me know
she is not playing around, and I nod.
I want to say, *Of course,*
I am loving as hard as I can, but the truth is
I still protect myself with Plans B, C and D:
if you die or leave me I'll move to Portugal,
adopt a dozen kids,
or go meditate in an ashram
until I see God face to face.
Carla's hair is copper,
her eyes a dappled greenish brown.
Oh damn, I can't remember
exactly what color her eyes are, even now while she's alive
and planning her own funeral, just across town.
I love you, I tell her, possibly
the lamest three words on the planet since
contrary to myth and legend they cannot cure the common cold
let alone what she's got. There's a moment
inside our moments, like a seed inside a fruit,
that is the only real thing. And we're just
grazing the husk of that, most of the time.
Carla's lit gaze is an arrow.
It shoots right through me
into the face of the sun.

Because even the word *obstacle* is an obstacle

Try to love everything that gets in your way:
the Chinese women in flowered bathing caps
murmuring together in Mandarin, doing leg exercises in your lane
while you execute thirty-six furious laps,
one for every item on your to-do list.
The heavy-bellied man who goes thrashing through the water
like a horse with a harpoon stuck in its side,
whose breathless tsunamis rock you from your course.
Teachers all. Learn to be small
and swim through obstacles like a minnow
without grudges or memory. Dart
toward your goal, sperm to egg. Thinking *Obstacle*
is another obstacle. Try to love the teenage girl
idly lounging against the ladder, showing off her new tattoo:
Cette vie est la mienne, This life is mine,
in thick blue-black letters on her ivory instep.
Be glad she'll have that to look at all her life,
and keep going, keep going. Swim by an uncle
in the lane next to yours who is teaching his nephew
how to hold his breath underwater,
even though kids aren't allowed at this hour. Someday,
years from now, this boy
who is kicking and flailing in the exact place
you want to touch and turn
will be a young man, at a wedding on a boat
raising his champagne glass in a toast
when a huge wave hits, washing everyone overboard.
He'll come up coughing and spitting like he is now,
but he'll come up like a cork,
alive. So your moment
of impatience must bow in service to a larger story,
because if something is in your way it is
going your way, the way
of all beings; towards darkness, towards light.

Say Yes to the Dress

a reality television show,
viewed while flying across country

And in this episode, a woman of forty-five
whose face says This cake is stale,
whose face says Just tell me
how much it costs, whose face, if you knew how to feel
would make you over-tip your waitress—
this woman, hauling her two teenage daughters,
her mother, her sister, and an aunt, announces
she wants to walk down the aisle in a ball gown:
festooned in something poufy, like Cinderella.

Even though the entourage and saleslady and everyone agrees
a middle-aged bride should wear a sheath,
something knife-like and discreet and lethal;
even though she and her fiance were both recently laid off,
and she's been living with this guy for years,
arguing about bills and laundry,
they have children together, they have a house
which they might lose and God knows
why they're even getting married now, neither one
has health insurance—still. It's her One Big Day
and she's determined to have it,
so dress after dress is trotted out,
tea-length confections of satin and tulle,
strapless numbers, ribboned and ruched,
and the words shirred, and scalloped and pin-tucked are used—
and found wanting.

The saleslady is practically drowning
in a magnificent tumble of glossy, rejected fabrics,
leaving the viewer to imagine the texture
of this woman's disappointments.
Her lower lip trembles,
she only has two thousand dollars to spend
(which in the parlance of this show, is peanuts).
Still, a girl has a right, doesn't she? Doesn't she?

The flight attendant trundles by
offering coffee and cookies and headphones,
and I'm thinking
Say yes! Yes, yes, yes already
to the sacred, dreaded threshold,
yes to being shredded like a negligee and scattered like seed pearls—
and we're a mile up in the sky where even in June
there's a frieze of lacey snow over the rough brown breasts of the
Rockies.
The plane tilts and rights itself so quietly
we don't even notice, dozing as we are,
in a hive of white noise,
suspended, blind, over the deserts and mountains
and fruited plains of our inheritance: Americans,
with not quite enough leg room
frowning or chuckling in front of our separate screens,
entitled to our dreams and dreaming them

Dust

A kid you teach at Juvenile Hall tells you his father is on Death Row. You carry the story inside you and it comes out three days later over glasses of wine, after we have finished the latest install-ment of Our Big Fight and are making up. It's a gray week when soup simmers on the stove yet the house never gets warm and bun-dles of dust lurk in the corners of every room. Now I carry that story inside me also: your student's father who has killed more than a dozen people. But that's not the point. The point is how through you and the hours you spend with this boy, sounding out simple words: table, motorcycle, release date, I touch the heart of sadness and hope. Remember, too, when you touch me you are touching the years I lived among refugees, speaking a foreign dialect, and the needles and thread and fried cabbage of my great-grandfather the tailor, eight languages rusting in his mouth as he pinned and measured men's trousers in New York. This letter to you only rep-resents my failure to hold street corners, stoplights, random passersby, the moon in all its phases cradled in my arms the same way we cradled each other last night. And you: cities, music, women, ladders and windows. Our dead skin is flaking away and leaving us, our cells changing and vanishing. More silver in my hair daily. Dust of our lives, eye-grit, detritus, we are too lost in its swirl to notice how many worlds there are within two people. And how, when those worlds touch, the whole web lights up, every twig, every strand, every molecule. And it was dust we fought about so bitterly; dust on the piano keys, under the coffee table, insinuating itself into the computer, and in all the odd corners of this old de-caying house. Dust that makes the world and buries it, that may be vanquished for a day but always returns, creeping, seeping, too humble to be humiliated and thus invincible. Dust of our own sweet bodies, singing in their sweat and longing, illuminated in a stream of sun just for a moment.

What About God

The rabbi comes to visit. We lay out cookies and tea; tamari almonds, stuffed grape leaves and strips of sweet red peppers. I hide magazines, pick up clutter although the rabbi wouldn't notice anyway. He looks like a Poli Sci professor in his soft knitted cap, carries a laptop under one arm, asks only for an electrical outlet, takes 2 % milk, and tells us he won't sign the certificates of straight couples until he can do the same for his gay congregants. Fine. We sit on the sofa holding hands, and he asks us in the most neutral way possible, about God. What do we believe? His tone of voice, his face, his manner, all suggest it would be okay if one of us answered, "Blue," or the other one said "I saw God once in the Greyhound bus station in Chicago, bumming cigarettes off the loiterers who were stranded there, but I haven't seen her since." It would be okay to say, "God is dead. I sent flowers to the funeral," or "I danced on his grave."

Lee says, "God is beyond our knowing."

I want to say God is a cloud of our collective confusion. Humming, buzzing, like a swarm of bees. I think of God as an aggregate. A congregation of stars. An infinity of dust.

I say my conception of God has changed, is changing, from year to year to year. The rabbi raises a mild eyebrow. "Really? That's very stable of you. My concept of God changes from hour to hour like the weather."

"Ah-ha! You see?" I think, sitting back. "I was right. A cloud."

Moon River

I was so young I thought she made the song;
I thought it arose full-blown
from her mind and mouth as it was being sung.
It was the streetlight or perhaps
an over-abundance of moon
leaking in through the window-shades
in the kids' bedroom,
and our babysitter Valerie, all of sixteen herself,
her silky brown hair hanging about her face like curtains,
would sing Moon River to us,
if we begged her to, if we were good.

I was so young,
it was before poetry had sunk its gilded claws
into my mind's skin
and her voice climbed the silvery ladder without faltering,
until I could smell and feel
damp midnight grass,
and see the glistening track laid out across black water.

(Though I didn't know what "two drifters" were,
maybe snowflakes?)
"Off to see the world," she crooned.
"There's such a lot of world to see…"

Even now, decades later,
when I watch candlelight flicker over your face
as Orlando Gibbons' opening chords
swell and fill the room,
I swear I could steal away like that,
not caring if it was music, or love,
or the river finally taking me.

Rosy Road

"T'ain't no rosy road," is what she said,
the lady by the pick-your-own farmstand in Maine.
August, 1987; the sky gray and low as a mud fence,
cell phones and email not yet invented.
We were young then, we wore the shiny
unspeakably annoying patina of smug youth
that knows it will last forever;
clothes from Goodwill and a '65 Ford
hand-painted with day-glo peace signs.
We were on our honeymoon,
and happy to tell anyone who asked or didn't ask,
because then they would get misty-eyed and coo
and sometimes give us free stuff.
So I forget what I said exactly
but I let this old-time Maine woman know
and she looked me up and down,
my muddy sneakers, my wild-haired doe-eyed
mad scientist husband and my poet self,
the air we both had of having just been let out
of the game preserve where they keep naïve kids too long,
and she said tartly, "Well I've been married
near on fifty years. T'ain't no rosy road."
Believe me, we paid full price for our blueberries,
but now I had a honeymoon story to dine out on,
and did, a story that lasted
longer than the husband and always ended
in an explosion of knowing laughter,
at least among the married women in the room.
Because of course she was right,
they—we—would convey to each other,
not in so many words, but with an eye-roll, a shoulder shrug;
marriage is a fairy tale sold to gullible girls,
a skeleton dressed in a gauze veil,

a mild-looking mare who will break your bones.
And anyone with eyes could see
(I see now) how soft we were,
we two, how unprepared,
how scared. Yet years later here I am,
teetering on new high heels
holding my father's arm.
He's seventy-five, I'm fifty, and the path
before us is strewn with rose-petals.
Once again the bride, I bow my head
beneath the weight of everyone's dream
of beauty and happiness, including my own.
Under the canopy you wait for me:
nervous, willing, no longer young.
I float on roses
to get to you, cast the sacred circle seven times
carrying a bouquet your brother composed; huge, defiant,
homegrown roses,
scarlet, magenta, coral, vermilion,
nodding their big faces sagely, saying yes,
everything the old woman said is true, and yet
here we are; we bloom, wither,
die and come back
year after year, come back to love again.

Amber

Two long teardrops of it
graze my shoulders, coolly,
as my mother's tucking-in touch was cool,
nights she and my father went out
in the glamour of their long-ago youth.
How I held my breath then
not wanting her to go. She went
anyway; gone for good, eleven years now.
These earrings I've inherited glow
mellow against skin,
reflecting, refracting. Light of late
August caught in their elegant oblongs,
dark honey of the inmost hive.
And now they swing
awkward, out-of-place against
my wrinkling neck,
this wind that's always at my back.
Amber was her song,
her go-to color, wine at sunset,
peaches poached in fire.
How we live to rue.
How love refracted,
deflected, bounces back
catches me off-guard—how we missed
each other, she and I
even when she was alive,
so that now, all these years
later, I feel her as a coolness
brushing my collarbone,
a tug at the lobe.

.

Cashmere

says its own softness
in the sound of its name, the *cajzh*
sliding over the tongue
like a pansy's petal, only warmer,
the *mere* like the whisper of your first love's name,
something half-forgotten,
tucked away in the drawer lined with tissue paper,
redolent with grandmother,
she who stuffed nylons with dried rose-petals
and hung them from light bulbs to release their scent.
And why does this memory
drift back to me now? Because I want
that hundred dollar sweater, marked down
from a hundred and forty
but still way too much,
still out of reach as the touch
of my grandmother's cheek,
gone for decades now, her powder and woe.

Because I have never seen the cashmere goat,
bred in the hard-fought Kashmir valley,
goat who is neither Muslim nor Hindu,
she of the cherished silky, double-layered coat
deliberately picking her way
down the rocky path of the Himalayas.
Because I have not met the herdsmen
or seen the place where the wool is carded,
washed and spun, nor sat with the women, weaving,
or heard their stories and songs. Because I have not sipped
their smoky tea in the dimness of the hut,
or lifted my eyes to the ring of mountains ranging me
wondering why the work of my hands may fly
where I cannot, I crave the expensive sweater.

Or perhaps
it's the ancient cleft between worlds I want,
the agility of the goat's quick step,
the way she lives at the edge of a cliff
without falling off. Or then again it could be
the strength and softness of those unknown women.

Maria

always with a mop or broom or rag in hand
scouring, scrubbing, wiping, cleaning
in the women's locker room
while the ladies, soft rosy sweating glowing from the sauna,
haunches spread on bench white towel turbaned heads
ask Maria and Maria and Maria
have you seen my sunglasses, could you tell them
the far left shower's not working,
and about the jets in the hot tub…
always Maria fully clothed and sneakered
among the damp asking naked bodies
five months pregnant beneath the regulation gray T-shirt
Maria squatting Maria bending, jiggling the stuck lock with a
bobby pin
fishing a wad of hair out of the shower drain
with a mop a broom a rag a bottle of cleaning fluid
resting her back briefly against a wall
in the chlorine mists the damp fragrant harem
working all the overtime she can before the baby comes
and if the world turns on work
and if the world turns on a bobby pin,
a bar of soap, a tube of lotion,
if the world turns on grace,
if the gift travels between bodies
in the steam and fatigue of daily life among women
then Maria and Maria and Maria
thin strong legs, black ponytail,
holds the key, hidden there in plain view,
a broom a mop a rag in hand

Day of the Dead, Oakland, California

Painted faces glitter in harsh sun
and rough heels slap cement; the dance has begun.
On paving stones stained with phlegm,
by an altar trimmed with marigolds,
Coke cans, and bottles of rum,
under the wafting of sweet tobacco,
they stomp and shuffle in a consecrated circle,
the displaced mixed-race descendants
of Aztec, Mayan, Olmec warriors. Watch them
in leather wristlets and beaded skirts—
squat, leap, turn and whirl,
circle like planets around a swallowed sun.
Despite fees quadrupled at the junior college,
and brazeros on International Boulevard
waiting for dawn trucks, for the day job
which comes or does not come;
despite makeshift altars on street corners,
in front of altars of teddy bears,
heart balloons and liquor bottles,
they dance to bless the dead,
restless in their dirt-prison-cradles,
and honor the living, harnessed to earth like this:
feathers, bells, beads and debt—
stomping a way out of no way with each mortgaged breath.

Citizens of a Broken City

She's shuffling around the lake in flip flops,
pregnant belly hanging out
over the open strings of her sweat-pants
shouting into her cell phone:
"You just don't get it!"

Indigo twilight streaked with horsetail clouds.
I'm dogging her discreetly, wondering
what don't they get? Everything, probably.
What it's like to be lugging her particular load,
wanted or not, into the uncertain future

while above us the sky is doing its big art installation thing,
sunset's last flush lighting up the West
like those pink neon thighs outlined in shaky fluorescent
on the sign swinging outside a saloon: enter here
for the time of your life.

We're citizens of a broken city, yes
in a dying time, yes,
amid the general din;
improbable that we'll be saved,
still we keep hoping,

which is to say shuffling, limping, or whizzing along—
kids on skateboards and bikes,
the lady with the pink hula hoop
swinging her hips in wide joyous circles,
Chinese elders practicing T'ai Chi under a spreading oak,
all of us putting one
semi-discouraged foot in front of the other
while above us the absolute indifferent magnificence
abounds, abides;
from a certain perspective even our ignorance is dazzling.

Manifesto

I was the wild-haired girl by the side of the road,
thumb out, steering a jittery course
between terror and boredom.
Hours later, if you cared to look,
you'd find me rattling around
in the back of a truck,
carried headlong into the next thing.
It was just my luck
to have been born when I was,
on the cusp of a chaotic abundance,
and, as my sister said,
I was the fastest sperm,
or maybe just the most persistent.
What luck I've had since then,
to sleep in the wet spot,
to bruise easily, to laugh till I fart.
What luck that my heart splintered
into ten million silver needles
each one on fire to embroider
love-stained and *prisoner of the self*
on red satin pillows.
Lucky to live a lifetime
in the years between losses,
to lie awake at night, wide-eyed
with the doleful sirens and the restless mice;
to sweat a misspent word, to rue the past,
to have a past to rue.
Luckiest of all: to have yearned mightily,
and learned a little,
to have lived inside desire
like Jonah in the whale,
perpetually greedy and hopeful,
making a lifetime out of each mouthful.
And then to find you! Luck

at the eleventh hour;
undeserved, red-faced, panting,
an overworked guardian angel,
a messenger
from all we can't see, a note
telling us that love is real
was here all along,
a forgotten blue-and-green marble in our back pocket,
an exact replica of the living world.

2
DESIRE
ZOO

Carried Along on Great Wheels

Dear ghosts long-vanished into ash and gray city wind

I think of you

When someone bicycles by with a little seat on the back, and in that seat, listing perilously earthward, a two-year-old girl half-asleep

Sagging down towards the pavement, wearing a tiny helmet and carried along on great wheels

Sack of potatoes is what my father used to call me, joking, when he hoisted me up on his shoulders

And I loved it, loved seeing the world from that great height

Now bare black trees stretch over the lake glistening like a giant eye at the center of our city

And from leafless branches an explosion of gulls, winging in unison

Their furious texts scribbled on sky and immediately erased

The lives we dreamed we'd live, and the lives we actually have

Dogs on twin leashes, pulling us eagerly toward everything that flies

Anything Golden

If you drive out along highway 80
with the gulls swooping and cawing,
white-caps on the bay and sun
piercing fog with thrusts of operatic light,
dying seems like just another climax
after which someone will yell "Cut!"
and we'll straggle back from the scenery cliff
and resume our places, speak our next lines.
"The walls look like paisley; the ceiling's made of flowers,"
Carla told me, the last time I saw her.
I thought she might be enlightened now
she was so close to the horizon.
"Is it all just atoms dancing, like mystics say?" I asked her.
"And do you know things now?"
"I'm high," she giggled. "I love morphine!"
She'd been remembering us, twenty years ago,
so young, with our young first husbands,
having burgers in a little dive in Cambridge.
"When I think of the brilliance around that table," she whispered,
eyes wide in her knife-thin face.
"How beautiful we were and didn't know it."
About me she said that God
got something right for once,
"Because who wouldn't want your light in this world?"
Her eighteen-year-old son squirted mist from a spray-bottle
into her parched, eager mouth, which kept wanting to say things
though she had no strength left really. I could have laid
myself down there with them,
dying-not-dying all afternoon.
I could have said "Not yet!" And "Don't go!"
as I have said to anything golden.
Too soon my five minutes were up;
Carla had told me everything

she had breath to impart—
that we were beautiful, and most of the time
didn't know it, though every once in a while a needle
of light might pierce the fog we're always swimming in,
and that was what was worth staying around for:
not just to see but to be that shining.

Words for a Student

It is thankless to bear news
of evil; no one wants to imagine
much less be
that baby still in her crib when the man
enters with thick fingers.
And yet we lean in
when you read your story, because love
divided by damage equals all of our lives
not cancelling out, but rekindling
the small torch of innocence
to human music. You are a testament:
the wildflower crushed underfoot
rises again out of rockiest refuge. You wish
your story were other
and so do I, but this fire
accepts any fuel. Thin shaky voice
a wire strung between distant mountains.
Fragile pen, mortal paper. The story is
the gift brought back from hell, paid for
over a lifetime. No, it is the circle of listeners.
No, it is the telling.

Pig at the Mexican Orphanage

Either it's all okay or none of it is,
like the lonely black-and-white sow with the bristly face,

her sty filled with rotting corn cobs
and the deep irremediable odor of pigshit

halfway up the hill behind the orphanage.
Past the yard where kids congregate

by swings and slides. Past pens
of bleating goats and the busy hen-house,

I stopped to talk.
Pig you stink and I have no children,

I said. She snorted in acknowledgment
and came close, her wet snout

with its damp, snuffly nostrils like two black tunnels.
Perhaps if I had a grass wand

I could turn her back into a princess
and avert her fate of becoming carnitas or jambon.

Perhaps if I dared to scratch behind her ears.
There are those whose pens

are definite and wooden, and others
whose only cage is the leaden sky

of their own mind. Look here, in the exact center of my

divided heart where the blood
is always busy, rushing and returning,

where old questions lie
like quartered rotten potatoes

flung on the compost heap
to spring back new again and whole.

Tell me: when they weigh my heart
against the feather of truth

will it crash the scales like a hammer
to the back of a pig's skull

or float straight up to Heaven
like the shrieks of these children

which reach me, faintly, no matter
how high I climb? Bright sparks

from the welder's arc, they know the language
of foot and soccer ball, frijoles y tortillas, just as I know

abandoned may mean *alone, desolate, bereft*—
or finally free to feel everything.

As Close As You Are to Me Now

The elephant: six tons of unexpected grace,
seeming, in the heat-haze,
like a man shambling up to us,
a man wearing a loose, wrinkled elephant suit,
who knows it's all a game of dress-up anyway,
him in his heavy gray costume,
me in my sundress and hat.

We watch him strip leaves from a branch
with his sensitive, expressive trunk.
Everything in his enclosure is the same color,
rocks, dirt, elephant skin,
and of course it is too small for him
as our own lives are too small for us.

We pass the water bottle back and forth.
I want to offer it to him.
He is so human and present,
so calm and fathomable.
Then Mirabai caresses my upper arm,
eentsy-weentsie-spidering up and down
to where the flesh is sagging now, above the elbow.

Oh child, I am following in the footsteps of elephant,
gray and heavy-footed,
down the long dusty tunnel
to where I someday disappear.
And you, my darling, in your perfect skin,
peach-smooth and summer-warm,
are just beginning,

taking everything in with open eyes:
this desire zoo,
this flesh journey.

Watching the Giraffes

The baby giraffe stands
in the shadow of the tall mother-body,
both of their astonishing necks marked
with a perfect mosaic pattern
like kitchen linoleum.
The mama bends to lick
the soft nubbins above his ears.

How close the gods come to us sometimes,
how quietly.

Then an even taller one (the father?)
who has been gazing off into the distance,
his small head atop that neck
like a long lonesome train whistle
high above everything,
lets loose a Niagara of yellow pee
and another giraffe ducks
a swanlike neck down,
                         down,
to catch a deep, hot
mouthful of urine,

then undulates back up,
swanlike, elegant,
gulping and swallowing.

So that too is part of it.
How they take
what they are thirsty for
without apology,

as I am drinking in the gentle weight
of the child's small trusting body
leaning against my arm
on the bench at the zoo,
both of us watching the animals
without saying anything.

Marriage

1.
There we are, missing each other again.
My cherished collision.
My other other.
Your key fit my lock.
My rusty gate swung open.
Crying on its hinges.
My butterfly. My bruise.
My runaway dog of no known pedigree.
My long-lost life come limping up to greet me.

2.
I was thinking how much I love you
and yet we irritate each other constantly,
like a foot and its new shoe,
rubbing and rubbing until the blister pops,
then the raw ooze
on all that expensive leather.
Now it's winter and this blustery weather
makes me want to leap
into your arms like a large
ungainly German shepherd.
Trusting that although my weight
might make you buckle
still you'd gamely catch me:
our second date was at a skating rink
where, terrified and pretending
to be a woman of balance,
I started to slip
under the conviction I'd always fail at this—
you held my hands and steadied us.
Held fast through my hard staggering.

Though it nearly cost you your bones,
you would not let us fall.

3.
When she was dying my friend
tried to remember
to love every part of her life.
The taste of an apple
when she could still eat apples.
Walking to the toilet
when she could still walk.
The warm needles of shower-water
against her bare pink skin.
The friend who stood waiting
to help her scale the lip of the tub
when she could no longer lift her leg
those few last inches.

She tried to love the small
borrowed bird of her breath,
and the ocean which almost devoured her
the day she parked her wheelchair
close to the surf to say good-bye.
I told her a joke
and she almost choked to death,
laughing. Not a bad
way to go, she declared
when she could breathe again,
looking at me with such a fire of love
I could not bear it and turned
cowardly away

4.

I'm washing dishes
looking out at the neighbors' garden,
their cactus and corn,
measuring the season's flight
against the height of dry,
almost-toppled stalks.
Then your enfolding arms around my ribs;
my back rocks
into the crook of your torso,
we fit together like a wave fits water.
Perhaps we've had a fight
and this is the making up.
Perhaps it's just a moment when I know I've got it good,
and that's enough.
The sink's full, water's running,
warm and clean, over my working hands.

Feeding the Feral Cats

City yards
A series of weatherbeaten
Fences. Geography of
Piss and entrails,
Smell and feather.

Her clean, pink,
Diamond-shaped anus
Slinking away

Having hidden her three kittens
Under some stray boards

Whisk of black and white
Tail, bared teeth, yellow eyes—

Torn pink silk of an ear, paw-
Pad slashed and bleeding

Battered silver water bowl,
Dry rattle of food-bag,
Skritch of food-can opening,
Set out discreetly

Suddenly, a bolt of black
And white lightning,

Hunting or Hiding
Under the hulking metal bodies
Of parked cars

At twilight their stark dark shapes:
Totems

The luxury of loving completely
What will never love you back

unsolved

she was a girl who
needed a home and I
was four walls and a roof and a door and
she was seventeen and had been beat up
by life harder than a white woman
can imagine and I had looked over
my shoulder and seen forty passing by and fifty
zooming up fast and she
was a cell phone that talked all night
and I was call waiting
patiently on hold never giving up and she
was a bad debt and I was a checkbook
she was an open womb and it was
closing time at my bar I
was a stop sign and she rolled through me
she was being spit out of the centrifuge into the furnace
and I was being vacuumed into the void like dust
by that same inexorable wave
how can I tell you the story
magpie mockingbird cuckaberry sits in his old nut tree…
even now
her creditors keep calling
thinking they're going to get something, but she
is a hurricane of broken promises
and I am a warning:
look how your crooked tree
bears its crooked fruit

Fig Tree

Offering herself to strangers,
her ripe purple ova,
her sweet sacks of seeds
soft for the squeezing and tasting—
somebody tell her
not to do that!
Sprawled all over the sidewalk
for any dogwalker to finger.
Any old lady, hobbling by on her walker, gets one.
Or homeless guy settling in for a smoke.
Or surreptitious single mother
with her plastic bags,
her army of climbing kids.
Not very ladylike,
crotch open for a sneakered foot,
a panting embrace,
and all that black honey, oozing.
See how her heart's left
smashed on the sidewalk
for feral cats to sniff,
her intimate goo underfoot,
pecked by pigeons, swarming with ants.
Should have pruned her harder,
brought her up short
before she showed her desire so freely
upraised arms opening to sky, profligate
branches that could poke somebody's eye out:
such crazy need to feed the world.

Messed-Up Villanelle About Intimacy

You criticize the way I wash the dishes;
I left some oatmeal clinging to the spoon.
Neither can fulfill the other's wishes.

I didn't know how tight your mouth could get.
Your rose-lipped mouth, your sweet, your soft, your wet—
I say I'll clean the tub but I forget.

You're brittle as a pencil, made to break.
I'm soft as an eraser, dull and dirty,
Is this an epic love or huge mistake?

What cosmic joke are we enacting here?
What cruel god stuck two old fools together?
You turn from me and sleep on your good ear.

This marriage business makes for vagrant weather,
Although next night we're sweet again, and flirty,
And in the kitchen dance and laugh together

For love ferments a brew that's quite capricious,
And serves it up with salt from year to year,
Though neither can fulfill the other's wishes.
(I know this isn't what you want to hear.)

After the Fight

All day we tripped over the puniest of words,
hardening like lemons in the fridge
or soap-scum on the bathtub's ledge.

Having come this far and run out of rope,
at night we lay down our separate books,
turn out the lights, grope

each others' faces for a clumsy kiss.
Follow the sound of my voice, you joke,
a thin thread of tenderness.

Sorry for what I said. This
being like Arctic explorers, yoked
together, blind in the blind abyss

scaling the lip of the glacier's great nothingness;
if one falls, the other perishes, so
even asleep on your good ear, my voice

seeks you out, (hushed, frayed, hesitant),
mumbling love groans and gibberish
dream-speech, finger-touch,

seeking to redress
the ancient catastrophes, fault lines
that are no one's fault anymore,

fissures
we cover with a caress;
fragments which may someday coalesce.

Napa Wine-Tasting

I confess I'd hoped for hay,
and maybe some crushed grape-skins on the floor,
a barrel full of stomping virgins,
with goats, perhaps,
or at least a few chickens.
But the place is antiseptic, stainless steel,
the young woman behind the counter blonde and precise
as she pours us out our twist of white
and speaks of fig and melon on the tongue.
A few merry swallows and I start in:
"Impertinent, like someone in a French maid's outfit
begging for a spanking.
Richly deserved, I might add."
"Sssshhhh," you hiss. We try another:
"Ah, elegant, like an embezzler,
packing to flee to the Cayman Islands,
having drained his company's coffers to the lees.
He's wearing a tasteful pinstriped suit, and maroon tie,
but all he's bringing with him are Hawaiian shirts."
"Okay, enough." But with each pour I wax more eloquent:
"This one's brash, a young punk
on stolen hot wheels. Mmmm,
I hear police sirens. Taste that after-burn."
"Am I going to have to take you out?"
you wonder; meanwhile
the blonde slips us a velvety red.
"Oh honey-mouth! This one's a kiss
between good friends that turns to something more—"
"That's it, thanks, we'll take these three. No, four."
You pay, then grab the bundle, hold my hand
as I stagger, giggling, through the parking lot
and in the car, your dear
familiar lips: "Oh peach, oh spicy hints
of lilac and chocolate, oh stubborn, faithful star..."

Peaches

The eloquence of the cat's sinewy jump
to the kitchen counter where he knows he is forbidden
is different than the eloquence of an elbow shoving him off,
paring knife clattering to the floor.

Just as the eloquence of the green worm
slowly eating its way from the heart of the peach outward
sings differently than the pile of cut peaches in the bowl,
glistening in their juice like wounded suns.

The eloquence of the woman's weathered hands,
searching and picking and slicing through peaches,
their perfume rising, one part wistfulness, three parts honey,
is not the same as the eloquence of her husband's back stooping
to his work:
saw and sander, chisel and clamp.

His back: a shelter between hurricanes,
a question of metal and fire, an open door.

And then the eloquent silence of him looking at the laden tree
and his wife
going back and forth from the house
with the small stepladder and the colander full of fruit.
The gaze he gives her through which the hard season
of cold leafless branches has passed, and roundness resumed,

and the glance she flings back at him: one part rue, two parts amber
as she goes into the house and picks up her knife
and turns again to the cutting and storing and putting by.

White Lady of Once a Week

The child lolls half-asleep in the front seat.
"Why do it start and then stop?" The rain, she means.
"The clouds are banging into each other," I tell her,

which is what someone told me when I was her age, seven.
Turns out to be wrong, wrong again.
Like almost everything.

Her hair's in tight cornrows. In this light I see the downy fuzz
of what will someday become a mustache
she may bleach, or despair of. She's frowning.
Little woman. Unfurled rose.
"But why do it start and then stop?"
"I don't know." "You don't know?"
Clouds overhead, the color of dark bruises.

"I am ghetto," she says then,
so faint I almost don't hear her over the hip-hop,
which she's cranked, as usual
to the hundredth degree of deafening on my radio.

It's always in the car when I'm picking her up
or more likely dropping her back home, that she says these things.

"What?" I turn the music down.
"Nothing."
"No—I heard you. What did you mean? You're not
just where you came from. You can be whatever you dream."

At that she reaches right past me
without a word and turns the sound back up,
as I deserve.

Okay then, White Lady of Once a Week,
Fisher in the Flood,
Mouther of Platitudes at the Apocalypse.

Wrong again. Wrong about almost everything.

the book of last year's resolutions

is fickle; each dead leaf
needing to be swept
and binned; then
the faded fire of the bougainvillea

like a rain from heaven,
like my friend
whose final breaths through morphine
were entrained to such a river,

whose voice was silver until it was silenced,
who found that finding a way
to leave this earth
even in a stripped, forsaken body

to be such labor, like birth,
like a god moving achingly through matter
before sloughing it off,
contractions of the shattered heart widening

in awe beyond the cloud of self;
so the book of life in which we long to be inscribed
has the thinnest pages
they disappear as soon as they are turned

Elusive

I love the gray and black striped cat I can see out the window
stepping precisely between furrows in my neighbor's garden

more than I love the white cat curled at my feet
taking up half this couch.

The cat out the window is lithe and mysterious.
I can see him move away,

tiger stripes into green grass.
The cat at my feet has been vomiting

clay-colored fur-balls
on the good red rug all morning.

So I won't ever be able to re-enter the dream again
and find where I hid the lost poem, in the crotch of a tree,

or touch the tempting two-day stubble
of the man on the train who wakes rumpled from his nap,

nor stroke the nape of the woman with smudged mascara
and a half-glimpsed tattoo of a butterfly

at her sacrum, just above the y of her thong;
a butterfly which flexes its shy wings when she bends over.

Say it was enough to have seen it once.
Say telling you about it now could be enough.

Domestic Violence

We are talking about the movie we saw last night,
specifically the scene where the mother
throws a TV down a flight of stairs
trying to kill her daughter, and then stomps back
to watch TV, only there isn't any.

Isn't that just like us? I want to say,
and you'll say What? Of course not.

Because literally we don't even have a real TV,
just the DVD hook-up, and no one throws things
except words sometimes. Which hurt like hell,
as we all know, but still.

Now you're bending the E string on the guitar, watching to see
if I get what you mean by the music,
when all I want is for you to fill this unfillable
hole in me.

But you won't. So pretend it's later. Pretend
I never said anything. I'm down on my knees, in the yard,
digging bunchgrass out of the roses.
The weeds hang on by tough white threads; everything alive
wants to stake its claim. Inside the house
you're working, composing. I said I'd protect your solitude

if it killed me, and sometimes I think it will,
but these are the promises we make when love has its way with us,
when it throws us down the stairs of our own will
and watches us stagger away, bruised but hopeful,
into the new world.

Language Acquisition

She has blossomed into complication;
my niece, not yet three,
has learned to say *either.*

I don't like the scary skeleton,
and I don't like scary pirates either.
In twenty years she'll be standing, head cocked,

in front of a rack of paint samples
saying *I don't really like the burgundy,*
but the rust is not quite right either.

And from there of course
it's only a short step
to *I don't want to lose you,*

but I don't want to be utterly consumed
by this love either. And from there,
and from then on—well, we all know

how the skeins get tangled, don't we?
We who are no longer little children,
yet not wholly grown up either.

Breakfast. Winter. 1969.

Icicles hung from the bird-feeders.
Thin sun couldn't crack the puddles' skin.
Girls still had to wear skirts to school.
The principal said so and he was God
and by God my mother wouldn't let me out into the world
looking like an unmade bed,
so Alberto VO-5 was summoned. Alberto VO-5
coated each hair on my head,
stiff as icicles, implacable as womanhood.

"Pain before beauty," she'd say,
yanking the wide-toothed, unbreakable comb
(which sometimes broke)
through the sullen thunder of my frizzy curls.

Wheatena. Half a grapefruit.
Brown sugar. Milk.
The yellow bus banged around the corner,
its wheels squeaking against rutted snow.
Four kids to cram into boots,
parkas, mittens and mufflers,
and though we were never really ready—
homework spilling out of backpacks,
the baby with his boots undone—
it was time to go.

The Boy, The World

The weight of the boy in my lap.
The boy with the bony butt,
whose coltish legs drape
over the loveseat's lip.

This boy who is just on the verge,
his round features broadening out,
whose day opens up like the seal
of a freshly-licked envelope.

Who smells of grass and dirt,
who smells of berries and moss,
who sleeps with his radio on,
who knows all the baseball stats.

Who strokes the hair on my arms
who is almost too big to fit,
who must leave for school in a minute,
whose elbow digs into my ribs.

Who squeezes my heart to a pulp,
who can't find his library book,
who runs out into the green world,
one sock falling down, one pulled up.

Old Paint

Sometimes he seems strange to me. I notice that his hair is thinning in front, that it poufs back a little, that he says "Yes, Ma'am," and "No, Ma'am," and even pulls out a chair a little for me at a restaurant, the way his mama raised him. I notice that he looks Southern, that he comes from different stock than I do, that his long legs are coltish and his body wiry, like a person who works hard all their life, whereas my people soften into middle age behind desks and reading lamps.

I notice his long fingers when he is working the power sander, gracefully curving figure 8's as he cleans the edge of layers of old paint, sending a fine spray of paint-dust into the air. He has a light touch, he's careful not to splinter the edge or wear away too much wood. His eyebrows and the ridges and hollows of his face are coated with white, as if he'd been dipped in flour. He looks like Abraham Lincoln, he looks like America: foreclosed farms, don't ask for hand-outs, keep a stiff upper lip. My people don't know from America. His hands are leathery with wear, with hard, skillful use. I watch him like a cat, this stranger in the backyard who shares my house and believes in self-reliance, who owns a sewing machine and a lathe and climbs into the other side of my bed each night, and I think *Who is he?*

Saving the Platoon

I wasn't there when they left you at your aunt's house
and went off to Alabama without an explanation.
Four years old, frowning in concentration,
organizing your Army guys
into phalanxes and battalions.
Who will comfort that fair-haired boy
with his full, trembling lower lip
zealously guarding the perimeter?
Boom! goes the big gun
and one of the green plastic GI Joes
goes down, but his buddies swoop in to rescue him
whereas no one comes for you
for days and weeks so you line up your troops
on Aunt Mary's living room rug,
jealously guarding your men from marauding girl cousins,
attacking and saving the platoon over and over.

Home Dancing

Dancing which leaves no trace,
like tears which have run their course,
and left lightness in their wake;
we dance when we can't speak
at the window by the place
a drunk left skid-marks last week,
crashing a stolen car.
You kiss my hair.
A feather.
Our feet are lighter.
You said dancing
with you must be like dancing
with an anaesthetized bear,
a rolled-up carpet.
Not true. It's an ocean.
I swim I swan I swoon up your leg.
Green wind touches light curtains
in the month
that promises pomegranates
but delivers rain,
and my body's wedged
into yours,
hip nestled into hip,
arm to waist-curve.
Moments like these
I want to die and leave no trace.
I want to go out dancing,
one small step left,
then moving lightly off
this earth
into whatever comes next.

3

HONEYMOUTH

Stanley Clarke

He's holding his bass like a bride,
bowing her softly, coaxing those little intimate hiccups,
those gasps and moans from her throat. Oh now he's
spanking her tenderly,
his fingers rapping her belly,
Chick Corea magicking the piano alongside him, and
I'm sorry, Chick, we love you brother,
but you look like a friendly science teacher,
whereas Stanley Clarke, his eyes half-closed,
has become some thousand-year-old
man-woman-third-sex-being.
The way he handles his instrument
you can see him in a New York apartment
playing while snow falls,
big white flakes: movie snow,
and the woman who comes in after a while,
and says, "Honey, don't you want to eat?"
her voice as smoky-sweet as barbecue.
And he says "Unh," 'cause he's so deep inside
the music he can't speak, but what else did the wife
or girlfriend fall in love with him for,
if not the bliss-blessed wound
that allowed this thing to claim him
as its voice. Then it's time for the gig.
He packs up and heads out.
After the concert
we're all standing and applauding,
everyone's on their feet,
and in the ensuing crush
my hand snakes backward
to your warm dry musician's fingers,
slightly roughened, spatulate
at the tips. Touch me so I know
where we are.

When I sprawl in bed in the morning,

he walks on my chest with his springy black legs,
stepping precisely down the breastbone
and
      over
            the belly,
as if I were a statue he had toppled himself,
as if he were a god, surveying the wreckage.

Then turns tail and paces
up my ribcage to the chin,
his sharp paws sinking in-
to soft flesh, each step a painful delight,
and pauses, inches from my nose
looking deeply into me with his green-yellow eyes.

This kind of love unmakes my mind;
unspoken, unspeakable, and never fully known.

He is shy, a hoarder of pea pods
and rubber bands, stubbornly loyal.
On a whim once, he leaped onto my back,
was lifted like a conqueror and borne aloft,
only to hide himself for hours afterwards
in a pile of laundry.

He cannot tell a blanketed toe
from a mouse or a sparrow,
but attacks all with the same ferocious zest—
reminding us the word for tiger
derives from the Persian, "arrow"—
as he leaps madly on a shaft of sun
piercing through the blinds.

Honeymouth

Sappho, your
small, weathered
breasts, old
figs, the last ones
left on the tree

withered, immortal
soft as honey

       *

On a bed of sweet grass
I crook one arm
around your small

waist   touch
with an inquiring finger
that source

Tell me something
I don't know about love

       *

A throb
a trickle
spring melt
the old sweet roaring rush
ever-new

eye to eye now
we make a lovely odor
cedar and geranium
woman and woman

*

your bony arm
seizes
hard round the back of my neck

pulling me down to blackbitter
earth with its worms and beetles

busily
making holes in the shrouds of our best
poems,

*

and your fierce
sharp-breathed   kiss—

an admonition,
an entrance,
a wound:
                    this.

What Could One Say to a Dead Person That Would Not Enrage by Its Triviality

Roses with heads bowed low after last night's storm

And the path strewn with crushed petals, smelling of fish emulsion, honey and musk

Everything today was in honor of you, especially the mishaps

I emerged from the unisex toilet stall at the public gardens to find a burly male worker standing at the urinal; both of us yelped in unison

I swear I heard you ghost-snorting with laughter

The dance of the commode in your last year; hoisting you up to pivot around, down, then easing back to the hospital bed afterwards, trembling with exhaustion, banked by pillows

That I believe something goes on after our bodies disappear; that I don't believe—it doesn't matter because it was/is in this body that I loved you and love you still

Your slender white freckled hands, the ring you threw into the ocean, the curve of your generous mouth

The time a careless lover left me like I was the scene of an accident and you showed up the next day wordless with an armful of flowers

Best of all: those moments when I made you laugh—huge, bright, eye-watering

Sunset tonight the same color as those apricot-blush-flame-colored roses

Ecstasy

for Carla

How you would love
the six-year old girl with jack-o-lantern grin
and swingy red dress—
dancing by the gleaming black grand piano
with its open mouth and white teeth.

Dancing so hard she cries out
to her mother: my feet are burning!
but she can't stop, she's in the grip
of what's rising inside her,
red-winged and fierce,
with serious talons.
Six years old and already willing
to throw her whole small body
into the furnace of that laughter—

and now your death
moves in me too
like her ecstasy —
the way she twirls and skips
and flings her arms and lets the music
take her

The Witnesses

I could hear the Jehovah's Witnesses before I saw them,
two black women dressed in black,
conferring politely on the porch steps.
Gray stormy day, and me, self-under-employed,
still in my pajamas at nine o'clock,
reading The New Yorker.
I ran to the door to head them off.
"Thanks anyway, but I'm Jewish."
"Oh," one lady said politely. "Oh, okay."
"We visit everyone," the other added,
and I remembered my grandmother, back in the seventies,
marooned in our suburban home where she knew no one,
waiting out her latest bout with hemorrhoids or pneumonia
until she was deemed well enough to be shipped back
to civilized Brooklyn where she lived alone
in a stuffy rent-controlled apartment.
Eagerly she'd greet the Witnesses
who'd drop by every day to debate with her.
"God?" Grandmother would say,
all eighty-five furious pounds of her.
"Don't talk to me about God!
Where was God in the concentration camps
when Nazis tied the legs of pregnant women together
so they would die giving birth?"
The missionaries knew no decent answer,
but were game to stay and talk with her
which is more than I can say for the rest of us.
They returned and returned,
and so a bridge was formed,
one made of loneliness, fear and doubt,
God's favorite materials,
and something moved across it,
even if it was only the ordinary human traffic

of pretending to listen with half an ear
to another person's incurable despair
all the while hauling one's own tow-truck of sadness
from place to place, looking for a spot to park.
And that too is holiness. Call it whatever you want.

Sunday Morning

A pot of coffee. The Sunday *Times* half-read.
Cat stalks the curtain's shadow.
A breeze blows through my head.

Our table's set with coffee, figs and bread.
A loved mouth offered up for kissing.
How can you be dead?

You tried to tell me: Live! But died instead.
Live now. I drift like sea kelp gulping air.
A breeze blows through my head.

Some days are weighed in sunlight, some in lead.
A mocking bird, a car alarm.
Your freckled hands and silver voice now dead.

The crossword asks a name that means "unsaid."
Struck down. In blackest ink
I write it. A breeze blows through my head.

Grief unravels time. Your hair was red,
Your eyes like gray-green pebbles.
Please stop being dead.
Or else become the breeze that's blowing through my head.

Buffy St. Marie, I Love Your Howl of Anguish Because It's Real

Even her name tasted of snow,
and her voice was wild river whiskey
knocked down the back of the throat.

"AND IT'S REAL, AND IT'S REEEEAAAL
ONE MORE TIME," she growled in that unearthly vibrato,
shaking my small, plastic
suitcase-shaped record player.
I never tired of it; never got enough,
played the same song over and over,
all the furniture in our living room pushed back
so I could perform flailing imitations of drug withdrawal,
whip-whapping my young head around like a yoyo in a hurricane.

I am a wound crying to be touched!
I am a fragile sword, stuck quivering in suburbia's gray tombstone!

My father threatened to break the record in half,
and my mother, scared, slammed what doors she could,
but that voice of rust and regret seeped in under the threshold,
with its message of hell-and-gone, its molten insinuations,
and I was already out of my mind,
galloping wild over the moaning hills, strung out on a line of song.

Sex Work

You have a very youthful voice is what he said, not *your voice still has perky tits*

But I immediately thought of the possibilities

All I could do with my voice, which, it's true, is young-sounding, supple and lithe

Still able to make the heady journey from angelic to guttural in one slippery slide

I could do phone sex! I joked, because I did know a woman

Big-bellied and white-haired with a mustache, fifty if she was a day

Who made something of a living that way

Relishing the fact that on the phone she could be blonde and petite, a naughty schoolgirl, whatever was desired

And though she maintained she'd heard some sick shit in her day, I mean really sick is what she said

Still who doesn't dream of being that anything girl behind the drawn curtain

Stretched across her great brass bed, all tumbled in velvet and other people's fathomless longing?

Standing In Her Shoes

In honor of Wendy Davis' filibuster on June 25, 2013,
when she spoke for eleven hours straight in defense of women's
reproductive rights. During that time she was required to stand
without taking any breaks for eating, drinking, or going to the
bathroom, nor was she allowed to lean, sit, stray off topic,
or pause in her speech

Standing in her shoes,
means stepping up, in those precise
ladylike pink sneakers,
like a high diver climbing the ladder,
looking down on a tiny, faraway, aqua pool of silence
she will somehow dive into
eleven unimaginable hours from now,

and then beginning
to speak
       and speak
             and speak
                   and speak

and not rest from speaking:

Members, I'm rising on the floor today
to humbly give voice to the thousands
who've been ignored.
These voices
have been silenced…

Rising on the fifty-six small bones in two human feet,
tarsal, meta-tarsal, ball, heel, arch, and instep,

standing for hours as the bright flames start,
licking tibia, fibula, patella,
climbing upward:
sacrum, vertebrae, occipital nerve,
neck, vocal chords, tongue.

Enter that body now,
in the embrace of fire,
as each word becomes incantation
and the body of one woman becomes the body of all the women
in Texas: breath, breasts, brain, womb.

*I was too numb after the rape to even think about being pregnant.
By the time I went to the doctor it was too late…*

*I was supposed to be on bed rest, because of my diabetes; but I had
two other children and my boyfriend had just left…*

*I was told the baby, if it lived, would never speak or walk or even
be able to eat, but would have to be fed through tubes for however
long it survived…*

*I was only fourteen—my stepfather had told me if I told it would
kill my mother…*

These are the stories no one wants to hear,
hidden by skirts smelling of baby pee,
panties rimmed with dried blood,
maxi-pads stuffed down the wastebasket at McDonald's
    during break,
down to the last box of Pampers
and another week to go till the check comes,
turning over the sofa cushions, looking for nickels and
    quarters again

Standing in her shoes means standing in the broken flip-flops
and varicose veins of every woman
who ever thought she couldn't get pregnant
because it was the twenty-eighth day and her period was just
about to come,
because he said he'd pull out,
because he did pull out,
because he didn't,
because the condom broke,
because she douched with vinegar afterwards,
because she tried to kill herself by swallowing a bottle of aspirin
or made herself fall down the stairs
or punched herself in her own stomach.

Because these are the stories no one wants to hear,
she is reading them aloud, into the record, deliberately,
wiping streaming eyes, blowing her nose,
continuing to read through snot and tears—

I didn't know where I could turn...

*When the money ran out, I wouldn't eat. I would give the food to
my daughter...*

*I was working double shifts seven nights week, but when I passed
out in the Ladies' Room...*

Seven, six, five more hours to go

the gallery of the Senate chambers filled now
every seat in the balcony taken, the crowds amassing
and behind them and beside them and sitting on their laps—
the ghosts:

Madonna Of The Coat Hanger

Woman Who Drank Poison

Woman With No Face Who Jumped In Front Of The Train.

If it is in and through
the body that we come to know ourselves as human

If it is through women,

Through a particular woman

That we become the word made flesh made word
again and again

Witness then, O people!
Witness, holy ghosts!
How by a host
of beings-beyond-bodies
this woman is carried
out of herself
into history
speaking and speaking with the tongues of the silenced

Late October

When I see how our persimmon tree
is bearing so much thickly-clustered fruit,
the hard round orange heads, each with a star
of stiff leaves at the stem,
weighing down and cracking the branches,
I think of my friends who died young
with their unfinished lives still
thrusting and ripening inside them.
It's not true that God never gives you more
than you can carry.
Look how this whole limb has broken
under the weight of its own bearing
like a woman in childbirth
when the baby's head is too big
and the road too far from a doctor.
We want to think we can choose
between one kind of dying
and another. But something larger than will
compels a blanketful of birds, like tossed confetti,
to wheel in a great funnel shape overhead,
one last hurrah before they make for the Southlands,
necks outstretched, cawing and cawing.

Blasphemy

I'm sliding down. Forgive me.
Even as our little star is burning out
and a greater darkness crowds in,
even knowing love
won't let us off the hook, the rope, the nail
or save us from the task
of finding our own path to salvation,
and that to say "I need you" is a kind of blasphemy,
a swipe at the great American God of Independence—
still. You are the closest
I have come to knowing
the source of all life,
the center of the darkly turning wheel,
bright flare that kindles
the breath of every least being,
spider-web to cat's paw to the yellow shout
of sunflower. Oh, I was on my own for years
and could do it again
if I had to, could make coffee for myself and sit
looking out the window
as fog fingers the garden,
could find a way to fill the hours
now that you have filled me
with such music. And I know God
walks these hills alone, haunts
vacant lots and deserted beaches,
waits with the patience of a cat,
eats grief and joy with equal gusto.
But oh, Great Breath of my wandering days
and nights, I ask that you let me die
before I stop
drinking in this sweet green light
from these all-too-human eyes
that live with me now, tracking my small journey
through our fragile days and our vast dark night.

Sustain

1.
My love plays piano and his foot hovers above the pedal.
Sustain, they call it when the note floats
like a basketball player suspended in air,
or a question whose purpose is to remain unanswered.
There's this low keening urgency,
drone and descant, murmur and coo.
I am learning to rest inside the word *enough*
its rough leathery consonants, its *f* of finitude.

2.
To bear up under
pain, or the memory of pain
repeating itself, like scales, as if we were practicing
to never do again what
of course we will do again…

3.
I love you
the way language loves the tongue,
the way a sentence loves its verb,
and parentheses love whatever they enclose.
I love you the way notes love the fingers that play them,
the way the ear loves sound
as well as the silence that comes after.

4.
After divorce
we sustained multiple injuries,
head wounds, trauma, shock.
But you can't sustain shock.
You keep on moving, into deeper waters.

5.

Give us this day our stone-ground wholegrain toast with organic
    butter,
our fair trade coffee, our soy creamer, our free-range eggs,
our morning paper with its dismaying headlines,
our kissing and teasing in the kitchen.
Let it all go on, just
another day, or week, or ten or twenty years.
Barely enough time to slip through this life
like a fish through a hole in the net,
or a string of pearls through nimble fingers,
a lone saxophone note draped around the silken neck of night.

6.

When I was young I worshipped the spark
of the ignition, turn of the key in the lock,
open door, blank page, lost maps,
deserted freeways, and myself.
Me, with my thumb stuck out,
going for broke, coast to coast, on shredded brakes.

7.

Later, after the fire
had burned through and taken
with it my most cherished obstacles,
I learned to live in a field of ash, holding
sorrow when there was nothing else to hold onto.

So I don't know this woman
with the clean kitchen, the watered garden,
curly-leafed kale and immortal chard
growing around her house.
I don't know how
she keeps it going, sustains this note
we've put our weight on,
or how the trees keep on standing there

with all the trouble they've seen,
breathing in poison, giving out oxygen.
I want to be like them, although I am only
a flesh apple of hope and doubt.
I want your hand in mine,
as the old world ends and something else is born,
singing love's praises just a little while longer.

ACKNOWLEDGMENTS

"Sustain" was published in *Hanging Loose*

"Waking Up," "Love Shack," "Dust," "Because even the word obstacle is an obstacle," "What about God?" "Anything Golden," "White Lady of Once a Week," "Citizens of a Broken City," "Because these failures are my job" and "The Witnesses" have been or will be published in *The Sun*

"Messed-Up Villanelle About Intimacy" in *Oberon*

"Rosy Road" in *The Atlanta Review*

"Say Yes to the Dress," in *Rattle*

"Man on Wire, Woman On Couch Screaming" in *Prairie Schooner*

"Pausing Before Plunging In" and "Honeymouth" in *Bluestem*

"Home Dancing" in *Your Daily Poem*

"Stanley Clarke" in *Poeisis*

"Domestic Violence" and "Moon River" were both long-listed for the Montreal International Poetry Prize 2011 and published in their anthology.

"Carried Along on Great Wheels," "Pig at the Mexican Orphanage," "Amber," "Cashmere" and "the book of last year's resolutions" were all long-listed for the Montreal International Poetry Prize 2013 and published in their anthology.

"unsolved" in *Handful of Dust*

"Fig Tree" in *PoetryMagazine.com*

"Maria," "Breakfast. Winter. 1969"and "Buffy St. Marie" in *Clover*

"After the Fight" in *Syracuse Cultural Workers Women Artist Datebook 2014*

THANK YOU TO MY FATHER AND STEPMOTHER, David and Samyadevi Luterman, for being both hearth and lighthouse. You are both my most beloved and respected spiritual teachers. Also, always: Dan, Emily, Jim, Vicky, Sairey, Josh, Noah, Branden, Theo, Jarid, Eli, Anna and Lucy. And: Dave, Jon, and Leonie Sherman, and Chris, Moire, Fran, Margie, and Meaghan Carmody (and Laszlo and Liam, Seamus, and the as-yet-unnamed new little one). I love you all—thank you for being my family!

THANK YOU ALSO TO MY PATIENT AND EAGLE-EYED WRITING GROUP, who read innumerable drafts of everything: Rebecca Chekouras, Ericka Lutz, Leslie Absher, Dianne Jacob, Natalia Vigil, and Coke Nakamoto. Also, for moral and/or poetic support: Lisa Klein, Ellen Lerner, Beth Dickinson, Dave Lee, Alan Cohen, Sy Safransky, Angela Winter, and Tim McKee, Mary Senchyna, Susan Clark and Angela Shannon.

THANK YOU TO LAUREN ARI, whose beautiful wild art graces the covers of all my books, and whose friendship graces my life, and thanks also to poet extraordinaire Daniel Ari, and to their daughter, my goddaughter Mirabai Ari, many kisses.

THANK YOU TO LOREN LINNARD, Judith Kunitz, and Dean Linnard for artistic collaboration and friendship. To Kim Rosen for inspiration, vulnerability and depth. Thank you to Ruth Schwartz for soul sustenance through the decades. Thanks and love to Gerry Thrash. Heartfelt gratitude to Meridel Tobias, Anna Benassi and Taryn Thomas for helping us with love and skill.

THANK YOU JANE UNDERWOOD for keeping the Writing Salon afloat and me employed, and to Marci Rinkoff and the girls for laughs. Thank you to everyone in Interplay and Wing It! for playing with me, especially Phil and Cynthia and my sister-wives Leo, Beth H, Julie C and Coke. To Ted and Suzanne Hinman and family, overflowing love, always. Thank you Mark Hauber for poetic neighborly chanting.

TO MY STUDENTS OLD AND NEW for so many moving and hilarious moments around the writing circle—you have enriched my life more than you know. To Susan Harrow in gratitude for your good work and for letting me share in it. Thank you to our cats, Trixie and dear, departed Wheat Thin, for deigning to incarnate as minor gods of the household.

MOST OF ALL, OF COURSE, FOR THIS BOOK you are holding in your hands, thank you very much to Luis Rodriguez and the good people at Tia Chucha Press for your hard work, persistence, faith, and courage.

THE SPIRIT OF CARLA ZILBERSMITH, artist, mother, muse, and friend, hovers over this book, and blesses my life.

AND OF COURSE, FOREVER AND ALWAYS, thank you Lee Bates, for your brave, tender, and tenacious heart.

ALISON LUTERMAN has written two previous books of poetry, *The Largest Possible Life* (Cleveland State University Press), and *See How We Almost Fly* (Pearl Editions). Luterman also writes plays and personal essays.

She has taught at The Writing Salon in Berkeley, at Esalen Institute and Omega Institute as well as high schools, juvenile halls and poetry festivals.

Check out her website www.alisonluterman.com for more information.